Presented To:

_____

From:

_____

Date:

_____

The Search for Peace
Daily Meditation & Study Guide

Published by

Black & White Press
Simplifying the Spiritual

"But words are things, and a small drop of ink, falling like dew,
upon a thought, produces that which makes thousands,
perhaps millions...think." ~ Byron

ISBN-13978-1467938495
ISBN-10: 1467938491

The Journey Begins

This book is designed to be a companion to *The Search for Peace.* If you have read Part One in that book you already have clear insight into why this Journey is mandatory. Because of a lifetime of wounds embedded into our souls, most of us walk through life with so much baggage that the dream of *PEACE* is little more than a dim, far away illusion. We love God and want with all our heart to live a victorious life, but we don't know where to start. Well, Beloved Reader right here, on these pages, is the place to start.

We are Created, Called and Destined to Walk Upon Earth as Powerful Women of God.

Father has a detailed Journey for each and every one of His *Little ONES* (His Daughters.) He is not trying to keep your individual *Assignment* a secret. Before the foundations of the world the *Plan*, as well as the *Provision* was set aside for you, no one else can touch it. Just as when God sent Samuel to anoint a King over Israel, that anointing oil couldn't flow on anybody's head except David's. What Father has set aside for You to do and be, is all yours.

I believe with all my heart, and it has been confirmed by the Holy Spirit, that by the end of the next Twelve Weeks you will have the knowledge and insight to begin to live the *Golden Dream in the Heart of God* for yourself. This has been a reality for many many other women…it can be your reality.

Because you have read (or will read) The Search for Peace you can identify with the writer Katherine Paterson when she wrote …*"Part of the magic of books is that they allow us to enter imaginatively into someone else's life. And when we do that, we learn to sympathize with other people. But the real surprise is that we also learn truths about ourselves, about our own lives, that somehow we haven't been able to see before."* I am confident this *has, or will happen to you as we continue this Journey together.*

The Search for Peace was born out of my personal journey to peace. It was given birth to for you. Sometimes as I am moving through my days *Practicing the Presence of God* listening for the still small voice, I hear Him say the most remarkable thing. He say's, *"You know...there is nothing I won't do for you."* My heart leaps every time He says it...I sometimes answer, "Oh Father I know! But what can I do for You?" More and more during the last few years His answer has been, *"Write."* So I write... because Father said so... because Father wants all children free...because *Now* is the time we must make the *Quality Decision* to be who we are and do what we have to do.

The Search for Peace is only a map. The really important book is the one you are holding in your hand and you will write it. On these pages you will document your own personal *Journey to a Place Called Peace*. I know this will work for you 'if' you do each assignment as directed. I say this without the least bit of pride, because in reality I am just passing on a message. Bear with me for a moment if I sound like an older sister and simply say, "Father said so."

As I have taught these concepts over the years I have come to know that some people will 'get it' and some won't...the one's who 'get it' fastest are the ones who do the assignments. Simply because they are willing to invest in their healing. As always the decisions is yours...a whole new life is only one decision away.

Don't wait until everything is just right.
It will never be perfect. There will always be
challenges, obstacles and less than perfect
conditions. So what. Get started NOW.

With each step you take, you will grow stronger
and stronger, more and more skilled, more and
more self-confident and more and more successful.
Mark Victor Hansen

A Gentle Reminder

As we begin the assignments lets talk a bit about the single most important aspect of becoming whole....what God says about us.

Most of us embrace the fact that we were created by God and that the Bible is the Word of God. That being the case… then the One (God) who designed the creation (Us) in the first place, would also know how the creation was suppose to work and He would include that vital information in the owners manual (the Bible).

I believe the Word of God is God speaking to us personally. Part of the assignments are to find a scripture and take it out of 'religious' language and paraphrase it into the language of 'reality'. I call it the Word, *"Up Close and Personal."*

Up Close and Personal and is not to be considered a true translation from the oringinal language of the Bible. It is merely my personal paraphrase of the Bible wherein a reader is able to make the sometimes over spiritualized Word of God understandable as an interactive on-going conversation. It is grounded in my experience with a Father God who loves us. Nothing more … nothing less. I suggest that before you begin working on your assignments each week read the Selected Scriptures in your favorite translation, then read them *Up Close and Personal.*

At the beginning of each week's assignments you will find a daily meditation from the book of Ephesians written in this style. Please take them personally. Use them for mediation and to re-train your soul into seeing yourself as God sees you and personally possessing all He has provided for you.

As each week progresses and you are working on your assignemts re-read the weekly scripture. It will change your thinking, and that my friend will change your life!

So Now it Begins ... Enjoy the Journey!

A New Beginning

We must be willing to get rid of the life we
planned, so as we can have the life waiting for us.

Joseph Campbell

~

You are never too old to set another goal or
to dream a new dream.

Les Brown

~

How can we be really living if we don't grow?
If we are to grow, we must be prepared to change.

~

The beginning is always today.

Mary Wollstonecraft

Now you are truly ready for the Journey. I hope
you will sign the Commitment to Myself...

YOU are worth it!

A Commitment to Myself

I understand I am undertaking the first Part of an intense guided Journey toward my own Reality… My Call… My Mission…My Personal Assignment.

I further understand that this commitment includes daily and weekly readings, meditations, and exercises that I will complete…even if my soul (mind, will, and emotions) have a fit.

I understand this course may raise issues, emotions, and truths that have been buried for a very long time. But I am determined to know the truth and the truth I know will set me free.

I commit for the duration of this course to the non-negotiable disciplines of spending time daily Practicing the Presence of God and writing the prescribed Word assignments.

I realize this is a Commitment to Myself and I am serious enough about wanting More, that I fully intend to keep it.

Your Signature_____

Date_____

Meditation for Week One

Ephesians 1:1-12 (Up Close and Personal)

This is Father's Opinion of You…as well as His Promises to You

Beloved Child,

Just like Paul wrote to the Ephesians, You are consecrated and set apart for Me. You too are faithful and loyal and steadfast. My grace, favor, and Peace (harmony, unity and undisturbness) are Yours. It's a free gift from My Son and Me. He paid for it and I give it to You, no strings attached.

I have blessed You in Christ, with every Holy Spirit owned blessing in Heaven. In My love I chose You…actually picked you out for Myself before the foundation of the world, so You could be blameless in My sight…You live above reproach, before Me in love. I planned in love for You to walk on the earth as My very own child…simply because it pleases Me and it is My will. So You could live a life full of grace, favor, and mercy…which I freely gave You when You accepted My Beloved Son Jesus.

In Him You have redemption, deliverance, and salvation through His blood…because of Him I see nothing but perfection in You. My love is gracious and generous and I have lavished it upon You in every kind of wisdom and understanding and practical insight.

I have made known to You the mysterious secrets of My will, My plan, My purpose for Your life in Jesus. It is in Him that You find out who You are and what You are living for. A long time before You ever heard of Christ I had My eye on You and had a design for Your Glorious Life…this is part of the overall purpose that I am working out in everything and everyone. That You might live a wonderful LIFE.

Love, Father

Week One

The Kingdom of the Soul

The Crystal Cup

I hold out to you my soul
An empty crystal cup
Praying you will
Fill it with kindness
With good …with love

I watch your eyes
Searching your heart
Weary of what you might
Place in the recesses
Of …my emptiness

I wait… hand trembling
For your decision
What will it be this time?
Life or death?
Light or darkness?

Week One Assignments

Check out Hebrews 4:12. It clearly states exactly what we need to tell the difference between the soul, the spirit and the body.

"For the <u>Word of God</u> is quick, and powerful, and sharper than any two edged sword piercing even to the <u>dividing</u> asunder of <u>soul and spirit</u> and of the joints and marrow (body), and is a discerner of the thoughts and intents of the heart." KJV

In layman's terms this means: As we study the Word of God it is powerful (able) to divide, separate; make a distinction between our soul (where we store all the 'stuff') and our spirits where the Holy Spirit, our Divine Guide lives.

Go back and read the samples of the negative core beliefs. Do any of them ring a bell? Note which ones.

_____

_____

_____

_____

_____

_____

_____

_____

When you want to step out of the box what do you 'hear' from the past that stops you? When and from whom did you first hear this voice?

_____

_____

_____

_____

_____

_____

_____

_____

_____

_____

_____

As a child what was your relationship with your earthly father?

_____

_____

_____

_____

_____

_____

_____

_____

_____

Is it possible that your past experience colors how you feel about a Heavenly Father? Any thoughts? Good or Bad...

_____

_____

_____

_____

_____

_____

_____

_____

_____

_____

Note: For years I only talked to Jesus...that Loving Heavenly Father deal was beyond me. Then I got to know Him. That's when I found true Love. Wanda

The Word Up Close and Personal

Write John 3:16, make it personal to you...

Sort of like... "For God so loved _____ (insert your name). Think out of the box...

_____

_____

_____

_____

_____

_____

_____

_____

_____

_____

_____

_____

_____

_____

_____

_____

_____

_____

_____

Practice

Find a few special Words in the Bible especially from Father and write them *Up Close and Personal,* **Psalm 23** is a good one. It begins **'The Lord is MY Shepherd I don't want for anything ..."**

_____

_____

_____

_____

_____

_____

_____

_____

_____

_____

_____

_____

_____

_____

_____

_____

_____

_____

_____

_____

_____

_____

Read them over and over this week. Speak them aloud, especially when you have a 'flare up' of a negative core belief. The revelation behind this exercise is the beginning of re-programming ourselves to think about 'US' the way Father thinks about 'US'.

NOTE: *You may be surprised and at times shocked when you do this exercise. What we are doing is taking the 'religion' out of the Word and inserting 'Reality'.*

Learning the Unforced Rhythms of Grace

One of my favorite scriptures that is sure to make you smile is from **The Message Bible.** Makes a great meditation as we begin the Journey.

"Are your tired? Worn out? Burned out on religion? Come to me. Get away with me and you will recover your life. I'll show you how to take a real rest. Walk with me and work with me——— watch how I do it. Learn the unforced rhythms of grace. I won't lay any thing heavy or ill fitting on you. Keep company with me and you will learn to live freely and lightly." **Matthew 11:28-30**

Practicing the Presence: Each day this week set aside five minutes to get totally alone and talk to Father. Say anything you want. He is not going to fall off the throne even if you're mad, sad, glad, bad, fed up or think this whole exercise is stupid. He is your Father, and He is like no other father you have ever met.

When your life is filled with the desire to see the holiness
in everyday life, something magical happens:
Ordinary life becomes extraordinary, and the very process
of life begins to nourish your soul.

Rabbi Kushner

After you have spoken what is in your heart (do it in every-day words just as you would talk to a friend)...listen to the still small voice inside your spirit...The Spirit Voice will come out of your mid-section not your head. He is there (in your human spirit) to tell you everything you need to know.

Expect Him to communicate to you...He will. How do you feel about this?

_____

_____

_____

_____

_____

_____

_____

Meditation for Week Two

Ephesians 1:13-23 (Up Close and Personal)

Use this week's Scriptures as a Prayer of Thanksgiving...

as you pray His Word back to Him.

Dear Father,

When I heard the truth and believed it, I found myself home... signed, sealed, and delivered by the Holy Spirit. The Holy Spirit in my spirit is a promissory note, a down payment, from You that I will get everything You have planned for Me. I have been destined and appointed to live for the praise of Your glory.

Father, I know that all this energy that is working in, and for me, is the same power You used when You raised Jesus from the dead and seated Him on a throne in high heavens, in charge of running the whole universe, everything is under His power. There is nothing anywhere... at any time that is not subject to Him. His is the final word.

Thank You Father for the utter extravagance of Your work in me…
because I trust You…You have sent endless energy and boundless
strength to get me where I need to be in You. Father thank You also
that I am part of the Church…and Christ uses the Church to continue
His Love Works upon the earth. I am a literal part of His Body. And
the universe must revolve around me…because it certainly revolves
around Him. I am IN HIM.

Love, Your Daughter_____

Daily Decisions Are Holy Moments,…
When we make them…
Heaven stands to attention.

Week Two

The Kingdom of Decisions

Decision Dance

I danced between the two

In 'Faith' Spirit danced with me

Playing celestial music

Choreographing my every step

Catching me when I leaped

In 'Fear' I danced alone

A black shadow

Standing in the wings

The music threatening

When I leaped…shadow laughed

Week Two Assignments

Read over the 'Commitment to Yourself'. How does it make you feel? Scared…committed…determined…empowered?

_____

_____

_____

_____

Do you have a tendency to keep promises to others…but not to yourself? When was the last time you broke a promise to yourself?

_____

_____

_____

_____

_____

_____

_____

_____

_____

Symptoms of a Soul Run Life

Honestly record your answers to the 'Twenty Questions.' Some of them may be honestly 'No', but if there are some 'Yeses' and a few 'Sometimes' you have just red-flagged a section of your soul Satan has been attacking.

Do I ever find myself being defensive or have a tendency to blame others for my problems?   Yes No   Sometimes

Do I have issues or problems with some people...all people? Yes No   Sometimes

Do I allow people to walk on me, or say unkind things to, or about me...abuse me?   Yes No   Sometimes

Do I have a need to control and have things 'my' way;

Yes No   Sometimes

Do I have to be right and try to convince others to agree with me? Yes No   Sometimes

When I am caught doing wrong, am I sorry for what I did... Or, am I sorry I got caught?   Yes No   Sometimes

Do I have a hard time staying in church unless I am in charge of something?   Yes No   Sometimes

Do I constantly need prayer and get in every prayer line   hoping this time it will work?   Yes No   Sometimes

Do I have trouble knowing it is God speaking...do I wonder is it Him or me? Yes No Sometimes

Are there areas in my past that still cause anger... pain... sadness... fear? Yes No Sometimes

Do I sometimes feel 'called by God' to straighten others out, or try to 'fix them'? Yes No Sometimes

Do I have problems with my finances, family, husband, children, or neighbors? Yes No Sometimes

Do I hide things from the people around me... food... purchases... secrets? Yes No Sometimes

Do I go out of my way trying to impress people with my... spirituality, money, or success? Yes No Sometimes

When an abuser from my past surfaces does my stomach gets that familiar knot in it? Yes No Sometimes

Do I have a temper...or compulsive habits such as ...mindless shopping... lying... escaping real life with too much television, the internet, or sleep? Yes No Sometimes

Do I lack 'focus'...am I going one way today and another way tomorrow? Yes No Sometimes

Do I have any addictive behaviours... drinking... smoking... over eating... drug abuse... illicit sex? Yes No Sometimes

I have a problem maintaining my healing, after I 'know' I am healed? Yes No Sometimes

Do I consistently year after year run into the same kind of problems... employment changes... failed marriages... money... strife... loneliness... rejection... illnesses... church hopping (this is a tricky one because we convince ourselves that 'God' is leading us on.) Yes No Sometimes

Am I afraid of failure... success... sickness... death... people... commitment... job changes, any change? Yes No Sometimes

Copy the 'Keys to Change'

You will find them in The Search for Peace on page 67. Read them aloud so you can hear them...

_____

_____

_____

_____

_____

_____

_____

_____

_____

_____

_____

_____

_____

_____

_____

Write down three things you have tolerated in your life that needs to be changed.

1._____

_____

_____

_____

_____

_____

2._____

_____

_____

_____

_____

_____

3._____

_____

_____

_____

_____

_____

_____

_____

_____

What can you do this week to begin the process of change? Write the Plan.

_____

_____

_____

_____

_____

_____

_____

_____

_____

_____

_____

_____

Spend ten minutes each day this week Practicing the Presence of God. Enjoy His Presence as you take a walk together. It's all about being 'God Inside Minded' no matter what you are doing.

You are my lamp, O Lord; the Lord turns my darkness into light. With Your help I can advance against a troop; with my God I can scale a wall.

2 Samuel 22:29-30 NIV

If words create reality.
And we are today what we
said yesterday....
What are we saying?

Meditation for Week Three

Ephesians 2: 1-10 (Up Close and Personal)

This is a Love Letter from Father.

Beloved,

Not so long ago you were running from Me, mired down in a life of saddness. You let the world, which doesn't know the first thing about LIFE, tell you how to live. You breathed the air of the lost one's and walked in disobedience. You did just what your soul wanted to do...just whatever you felt like doing. Never once, in all the years you did things your way, did I give up on you. With My Love and Mercy I kept reaching for you longing to embrace you. I took your sin dead life and make you alive forevermore.

I gave you the very LIFE of Christ and put you into a relationship of intimacy with Jesus and Me. I actually raised you up to the level that Christ has attained, because of what He did for you. When I look at you I see you seated right beside Jesus.

I did this because I wanted to clearly demonstrate during the ages to come the immeasurable, limitless, surpassing riches of My free grace, unmerited favor, kindness, and goodness toward YOU. I want everyone to know how much I love YOU.

You didn't have to earn My love…you don't have to earn it now. I LOVE YOU…because I want to LOVE YOU. All the wonderful things I have for you are yours not because of anything you did… they are all free gifts from Me. FREE!

You are My workmanship. I recreated you in Christ Jesus…born anew so that you can live the wonderful LIFE I have planned for you. Beloved, I planned your life before I created the worlds, I have marvelous things I want you to do…a good life all prearranged and made ready for you to live. It is time you embraced that fact.

Love, Father

Week Three

The Kingdom of Fear

The Habitation of Dragons

Paralyzed I saw him coming

A dragon of fear

Breathing black fire from hell

I took his flame

And started a fire of my own

Trying to thaw my frozen soul

And only succeeded

In getting colder still

Fear will produce the very thing you fear.

The same as faith will produce the very thing you believe.

Week Three Assignments

Copy II Timothy 1:7 Up Close and Personal *"For Father did not give Me a spirit of fear, but He has given Me a Spirit of Power, of Love, and a calm, well balanced mind (soul)...full of discipline and self-control."*

_____

_____

_____

_____

_____

_____

_____

_____

Draw a line down the middle of the lines on the next page. On one side write five of your biggest fears. They can be current attacks from hell, or the leftovers that burn into cinders every time they get heated up. On the other side write five *Up Close and Personal* Words from Scripture that contradicts those lies. There is a Truth from God for every single lie Satan whispers.

Meditate on the Word of God that He has given you to replace the fear filled lies.

Extend the time you spend *Practicing the Presence* this week by five minutes. Everyday this week **'for fifteen minutes a day'** be totally aware that He is THERE with you!

Record what you 'hear' Him saying from out of your spirit. Write 'Fear Tolerated...Is Faith Contaminated' ten times.

_____

_____

_____

_____

_____

_____

_____

_____

_____

_____

_____

Repeat that phrase aloud often through out your day... Replacing fear with faith is labor intensive.

Fear got us where we are..
Faith will get us where we aught to be.

Rehearse the answer instead of the problem.

What's Your Fear Factor? Pay close attention this week to where you tolerate fear. Note them in this Journal.

_____

_____

_____

_____

_____

_____

_____

_____

_____

_____

_____

_____

_____

_____

I have set the Lord always before me. Because He is at my right hand, I will not be shaken.

Psalm 16:8 NIV

SHE LEFT BEAUTY WHEREVER SHE WENT

Meditation for Week Four

Ephesians 2: 11-22 Up Close and Personal

Use this Word as Thanksgiving for what He has done for you.

Dear Father,

I want You the know I don't take all You have done for me for granted. It seems like I have spent years not knowing You. I didn't really know how all Your plan for my salvation worked. I lived so utterly apart from Christ…I was clueless! I had no idea about the rich heritage, promises, covenants You gave to Israel…and now, because of what Christ did, all those precious promises are mine!

Jesus tore down the wall that separated me from You. I am as much a part of YOUR FAMILY as the Jewish people! What a wonder! You have given me a fresh start…everything is new…Thank You… Thank You…Thank You!

Jesus came and preached good tidings of PEACE to Me…and now I have access to You. I can walk into the Throne Room any time and be welcomed…I am FAMILY! I have the same Spirit in me as Jesus did! How can I Praise You enough? I can't…oh, but I want to!

I belong to Your own household… I am set apart for YOU! The Kingdom of Peace is now my Homeland.

I am part of the Glorious Church! A structure that You are erecting, Jesus is the Cornerstone and all Christians are being welded together, by Him… forming a sanctuary dedicated, and sacred to You. We are Your Spirit Home. Thank You… for the honor.

Love, _____ (Your Name)

Week Four

The Kingdom of Hope

Hope

Blackness abounds as I kick through

The rubble of my shattered dreams

I see no future only the darkness

Of my lonely past

Then Father…in great Love

Picks up a fragment of my splintered self

Perhaps the one called…Hope

And gently…with care begins to build

A new Life…a new Dream

And this time nothing can shatter it

Because the foundation…is Him

Reach high, for stars are hidden in your soul. Dream deep for every dream precedes the goal. **Pamela Vaull Starr**

Week Four Assignments

Write down the things you personally 'Hope' to get out of this course of study?

_____

_____

_____

_____

_____

_____

_____

_____

_____

_____

_____

_____

Does the 'Chain of Command' in the war analogy make sense to you? Are there 'core issues' that may be stopping your soul (The Field Commander) from receiving clear orders from Central Command (The Holy Spirit)?

_____

_____

_____

This week add five more minutes to your time *Practicing the Presence*. Twenty minutes total... that will be ten minutes for you to say whatever you want and ten minutes for Him to respond... P.S. IF you ONLY said , "I love you," to Him...and you ONLY heard Him say, "I love you back," wouldn't that be twenty minutes well spent?

Do you recognize any 'snipers' in your life? By their fruit ye shall know them. Names? Did I mention this journal is 'private'? (;

_____

_____

_____

_____

_____

_____

_____

_____

_____

_____

_____

Note: Beware of well meaning but deceived people who under mind your decision to break unhealthy relationship patterns. They can create self-doubt in you and self-doubt can turn into self-sabotage. A 'Whole Woman' has no time to listen to negative opinions of herself. She has talked to Father and His OPINION, is the ONLY opinion that counts.

One Last Assignment: Look in your Bible for a scripture about 'Hope.' Write it *'Up Close and Personal'*. **One of my favorites is Psalm 39:7** *"And now Lord...I am ONLY looking to YOU... In You lives my Hope!"*

Yours ?_____

_____

_____

_____

_____

_____

_____

_____

_____

_____

_____

_____

_____

_____

_____

_____

_____

_____

_____

_____

_____

Meditation for Week Five

Ephesians 3: 1-12 (Up Close and Personal)

This is a letter from Father about your unique assignment.

Beloved,

Many years ago I revealed my Secret Plan to the Apostle Paul and to other chosen people. They then passed it on to you. This is the Secret I kept hidden for the ages... *You have your full share in all the riches that belong to My Jewish people... My Son's. You get the same offer, the same help in Christ Jesus. Everything I promised them in the Old Testament is now yours.*

The Apostle Paul did not feel qualified for his unique assignment ... but I called him and I qualified him. (My special Secret to you is...I have called you...and I have qualified you too. He had his special assignment...you have yours. I do not play favorites. What I did for Paul I will do for you.)

The purpose for these 'unique assignment' is that through my followers, all aspects of My Wisdom...My Power...My Love...My Grace would be made know. You, as part Me, are to take the Good

News about Christ and all He bought for them, to your world. Because of Him people can dare walk in boldness and confidence. They have free access to approach Me...I will not turn one of them away...they can all be in the FAMILY. So come to Me in freedom, never be afraid.

I Love You, Father

Week Five

The Kingdom of Secrets

If They Knew

What would people think if they knew our secrets

The secret tears we cry...the secret sins we hide

What if people knew the truth behind

The picture perfect family the picture perfect dream

What would happen if I poured it all out

Into the streets for all the world to see

There is no agony like hearing an untold story inside you.

Zora Neale Hurston

Week Five Assignments

This week we are going to take our soul searching a step deeper…as we go 'Back to the Future' you will need a **Separate Notebook** to write in…this list could get lengthy.

In your Notebook list the significant memories that happened between the ages of one and five, five and ten, ten and fifteen and every five-year segment until your present age. Write them as they are revealed we will be working with this list next week.

Note the answer to these questions as they apply, under each entry…How do I feel…where are my parents when these thing were taking place…who cares about what is happening to me at this moment in time…who was there making the brick that became a negative in my soul…where was God when these things were happening?

Soul Searching… Ask the Holy Spirit to help you recall things that might be significant. Don't worry about missing something, it is the Holy Spirit's job to lead us into all the truth…as long as we are open, He can do His part.

This exercise may be the most difficult one. Stand strong…you can do this…

A Reminder

"SOME REALLY GOOD ADVICE AND A WARNING"

When you are ready to recall the incidents that may have impacted your life, which are buried deep in your soul, do it when you are alone. Just you…your notebook and the realization of the *Presence* of the *Holy Spirit*. Ask Him to be there. Visualize Jesus right there with you, and or Father.

Please take a whole week to do your *Back to the Future* exercise. Do just one, 'time segment' a day. If the memory is just too devastating, *IMMEDIATELY* ask Father to help you…hold you, He will…good Fathers do that. Please also remember that you have *The Comforter* inside you…at your service. No one 'comforts' like the Holy Spirit.

P.S. Tears are okay…just call them liquid prayers.

Take you time. 'House Cleaning' is hard work…stop every once in a while and have a cup of tea and celebrate yourself…you are becoming a 'Sign and a Wonder.'

Add five more minutes to your *Practicing the Presence* each day this week. That will be twenty-five minutes a day…every day. Just sit there, sip your tea and let Him Love you. Talk to Him in your own words don't hold back, let Him talk to you, giving Him equal time.

_____

_____

_____

_____

_____

_____

_____

_____

_____

_____

_____

_____

_____

_____

_____

_____

_____

_____

The Spirit searches all things, even the deep things of God.

I Corinthians 2:10

Meditation for Week Six

Ephesians 3: 14-21 (Up Close and Personal)

Use these Words from Father as a Prayer this Week.

Dear Father,

Because of the greatness of Your plan for me, I come to You in the Name of Jesus, as I pray Paul's prayer for myself. Please grant to me out of the rich treasury of Your Glory to be strengthened and reinforced with mighty power in my spirit by the Holy Spirit Himself. I know He is in me indwelling in my innermost being and personality.

Through my faith I am asking that Christ be more and more at home...actually dwell, settle down abide, make His permanent home in my heart! I want my roots to go down deep into the soil of Your marvelous love. I want my whole life founded securely on Your love. I want whatever it takes to have the power and be strong so I can grasp, with the rest of Your people, how long, how wide, how deep, and how high Your love really is; and I want to experience that love for myself.

Father, I know Your Love is so far above my natural knowledge that I will need help to comprehend it…so HELP ME! I want to be filled through my whole being with all Your fullness. I want the richest measure possible of Your Divine Presence…until I become a part of the Body that is wholly filled and flooded with YOU!

I KNOW you are in me…Your power is at work in me and because of that You are able to carry out Your purpose for me and to do super abundantly above, far over and beyond all I dare to ask or think… infinitely beyond my highest prayers, desires, thoughts, hopes or dreams. TO YOU BE THE GLORY AND PRAISE FOREVER AND EVER!

Love You, _____*(Your Name)*

Week Six

The Kingdom of Forgiveness

Forgiveness

You hurt me

You took my last bit of dignity

And shredded it in my face

Calling me names I can't repeat

And then you laughed at me

You hurt my children

Took their innocence away

And left a wounded soul

Where children use to play

Then you said it was my fault

Yes, you hurt me

But this day I am Healed

I loose your hold upon my soul

As I hand you Forgiveness

I walk away in Peace

Week Six Assignments

List the people involved in your 'embedded image memory' exercise last week. Forgive and thank each of them. Remember you don't have to 'FEEL, like doing it. It is a *Quality Decision* you need to make for 'YOU' not them. If you need more space slip over to your Journal.

_____

_____

_____

_____

_____

_____

_____

_____

_____

_____

_____

Complete and unconditional forgiveness brought me soul-soothing peace and opened a door to a life I never dreamed possible.

Rosemarie Giessinge

By adding five minutes to *Practicing the Presence*, you will be spending thirty wonderful minutes a day, everyday with Father. Do something a little different this week...try *Practicing His Presence* as you straighten your house... read the Word...or another book...or drive in your car. Just *Center* into your Spirit and be so very aware of Him that 'He' is 'The Focus' of your world... because 'You' are definitely 'The Focus' of His.

Write down how you feel about *Forgiving and Being Thankful.*

_____

_____

_____

_____

_____

_____

_____

_____

_____

_____

_____

_____

_____

_____

_____

_____

_____

_____

Forgive Yourself

Instead of focusing on the things you have done wrong...the bad decisions...the goof ups...write down a few of the the things you have done right in your life. Yes, there are positive things to record. Look diligently...ask a friend...better yet ask Father.

_____

_____

_____

_____

_____

_____

_____

_____

_____

_____

_____

_____

_____

_____

A Point of Interest:When wholeness comes to a woman she gives birth to wholeness. It will be manifested in everything and everyone around her. When we want things and people to change around us... the starting place is within us.

Meditation for Week Seven

Ephesians 4: 1-15 (Up Close and Personal)

This is yet another love letter from Father

Beloved,

My desire for you is that you live a life that is a credit to who you are My Child, doing My business upon the earth. You have a Divine Call, a Divine Appointment from Me. I want you to walk out this Assignment with complete lowliness of mind, humility, meekness, unselfish gentleness, and patience. Pouring yourself out in acts of love toward others by helping other members of the Family along the way.

I want My Family to be eager to work together earnestly to guard the harmony and oneness that My Spirit in you wants to produce…It's called the binding power of Peace. There is only one Body, one faith, one baptism, and One Father. I rule over all, and work through all, and am present in all.

This doesn't mean that you have to be like everybody else. You are unique, and I like you different. My gifts of favor are given to you as an individual…your gifts are perfect for what I created you to be. Not only did Jesus purchase gifts for you as an individual, He went to Heaven and all the way to hell to be able to bestow special Gifts to the whole Family. He wants all of you to be filled with Himself.

The Gifts He gave to the whole Family were apostles, prophets, evangelist, pastors, and teachers…so that all of you could be equipped to do all the work I have sent you to do. These Gifts are to be used to help each other become fully mature in the Faith. I want My children to grow up in Love…until each of you walk the earth as Jesus did.

I need for you to stop acting like immature children, listening to everything that comes along with a 'religious tag' on it. You must stop being turned aside by every windbag, being taken in by smooth talkers. You must be so in tune with Me that nothing and nobody can take you in. They just invent ways to get you and your gifts. Beware! Beware!

Rather, as My child, you must let your life lovingly express truth in all things…speak truly...deal truly…live truly. Enfolded in My love, grow up in all ways and in everything until you are exactly like Jesus…healthy in Me…over flowing in Love.

I Love You, Father

Week Seven

Kingdom of Partial Peace

Almost There

A fragmented soul can fool you

You speak the 'Word' and it happens

You ride on the Glory of the moment

And even begin to think...I've got it

Then your limits embrace you

And you are at a loss to know

What to do… what to say

One fragment strong…another weak

But for that one brief shinning moment

You were 'almost' there

Week Seven Assignments

Are there areas in your soul you can recognize as not being right? Record any areas you know you need help with…allow the Holy Spirit to reveal others.

_____

_____

_____

_____

_____

_____

_____

_____

_____

_____

_____

_____

_____

_____

_____

_____

_____

_____

In the areas of your soul that needs renewing find scripture to help you with that process. Use the scripture in a love letter to Father.

_____
_____
_____
_____
_____
_____
_____
_____
_____
_____
_____
_____
_____
_____
_____
_____
_____
_____
_____
_____
_____
_____

Remember: This is a 'process' and the end of the quick fix so be kind to yourself...you can do this!

You are spending thirty minutes a day every day with Father...if you haven't already add a few minutes more...say five.

This week begin writing your *Morning Pages*. Use your other Notebook so that you will have plenty of space.

A Reminder: *Morning Pages* are a form of prayer. As you are diligently writing 'whatever' if a prayer request...a thought about your children...mate...scripture comes...write it. Write any and everything that crosses your mind in the morning...even distractions from Satan. If they are on the page they are off your mind and out of your soul.

Strip yourself of your former nature (put off and discard your old un-renewed self) which characterized your previous manner of life and becomes corrupt through lusts and desires that spring from delusions; And be constantly renewed in the spirit of your mind (having a fresh mental and spiritual attitude. Ephesians 4:22-23 AMP

Meditation for Week Eight

Ephesians 4: 17-32 (Up Close and Personal)

This is a Word of caution from Father about being deceived.

Beloved,

This is a solemn letter…but it is time you stop following the world's thinking. They have refused to follow Me for so long, that they have lost touch not only with Me, but with reality itself. They just follow the emptiness of their souls and the futility of their minds.

Their moral understanding is darkened and their reasoning is beclouded. They have removed themselves from the Life that is in Me. They want no share in it. This is because of the ignorance that is deep-seated in them. Due to their hardness of heart they have become insensitive to what is moral.

In their spiritual apathy they have become callous and past feeling, and reckless, and have abandoned themselves as a prey to Satan, who is full of every form of impurity and who fills their souls with depraved desires.

That is not the life for My Family! That is not the way Christ showed you. I know you are Mine and because you have accepted the sacrifice Jesus made for you, you must strip yourself of all that may be hanging on to you from your past way of life. Put off, discard your old un-renewed self, your mind, will, and emotions. You once lived like that but no more! You do not have the old excuse of ignorance, everything, and I do mean everything has got to go. My people are deceived because they refuse to let go of the past and to re-new their minds with My Word.

Get rid of the past and old ways of thinking! Take on and embrace an entirely new way of LIFE…a Father Centered Life. Fill your soul with Me. My Word. My Presence. This re-programming of your inner self will then begin to work its way into your everyday conduct until My character is reproduced in you.

What this adds up to is no more lies, no more pretense, no more excuses. You are a vital part of the Family…what hurts them hurts you. Don't hurt each other. When you get angry, don't sin; don't allow anger to possess you. Get rid of it before you go to bed at night. Do not let Satan find any un-cleanness in you. If he can find nothing in you he can't deceive you. Don't try to make ends meet by stealing. I will help you get a job so you can help others who can't work.

Watch the way you talk. Let no foul, or polluting language, nor evil word, or unwholesome, or worthless talk ever come out of your mouth. But only speak what is good, beneficial to the spiritual progress of others. Speak words that fit the need and the occasion. Let every word be a GIFT to the hearer…a blessing that expresses My Love for them.

Don't grieve My Holy Spirit Who lives in you. Don't break My heart by the way you live and talk. Let all bitterness, anger, bad temper, resentment, quarreling, slander, evil speaking, abusive, or ugly language forever depart from you. Get rid of spiteful behavior. Make a clean break from all the worlds ways.

As My Child I know you are becoming useful and helpful and kind to people. Tender hearted compassion, understanding and loving-heartedness is now your way of life. Forgive people for their past the same way I forgave you of your past. Act like Who you are…' MY CHILD!'

I Love You, Father

Week Eight

The Kingdom of Deception

He comes as an angel of light

A spark dropped into the darkness of our lives

A voice soothing…soft…persuasive

We take his words depositing them one by one

Into our wounded past creating a false hope

Blindness sets in as the evil is developed

It begins in our ear then slowly moves inside

As it is meditated into our fragmented souls

The angel of light whispered to us

'He sent me…He wants this for you…it's okay.'

We didn't know he was a messenger sent

From the evil prince of the dammed

We didn't see his shinning robe of light

Was only a cover for a shroud of darkest death

We didn't see the inferno blazing in his eyes

Nor detect his fiendish grin when he turned away

As we willing stepped forth in deception

At his bidding and do the unthinkable

Week Eight Assignments

Spend some quality time this week just sitting in His presence and praying for others, as well as yourself, family, and church.

Put a guard over your soul by writing in your Journal Word Prayers from the Psalms and other scripture. Sincerely pray and meditate on them until they begin to flow over onto your *Morning Pages*. That is when we know that our mind has been renewed to these truths. Remember we must have a rock solid base of the Word of God to insure us that we will not be deceived.

Such as:

Joshua 22:5 "I will serve God with all my heart and soul."

Joshua 23:14 "I know in all my heart and all my *soul* that not one thing has failed of all the good things that Father has promised me. All will come to pass for me not one thing will fail."

Psalms 62:1-2 "For God alone my *soul* waits in silence: from Him comes my total Salvation…(*for my spirit, soul and body.*) He is My Rock and My Salvation: My Defense and My Fortress. I shall not be greatly moved"

In this Psalm we are talking to our soul: an excellent idea.

Psalm 62:5 "Soul, wait only upon God, silently submit to Him; for my hope and My expectation is in Him."

Be sure to write your *Morning Pages* every morning just to gage what your soul is up to. With all the things we have been learning about the enemies tactics…we must be alert.

How did the information gathered in the Kingdom of Deception affect you? Write it down…discuss it with a friend or study group… tell Father.

_____

_____

_____

_____

_____

_____

_____

_____

_____

Jesus said in John 14:30 "The prince of this world comes but he finds no place in me." When the evil prince comes to us (and he will)…will he find a place?

Strongholds in the Mind

We must defend our mind against thoughts of deception. Only the Word of God can do that… II Corinthians 10:4-5 AMP

"For the weapons of our warfare are not physical (weapons of flesh and blood), but they are mighty before God for the overthrow and destruction of strongholds. (Inasmuch as we) refute arguments and theories and reasoning and every proud and lofty thing that sets itself up against the (true) knowledge of God; and we lead every thought and purpose away captive into the obedience of Christ.

Thoughts come to our mind, (which is a function of our soul.) When a thought comes that tries to go above the Word we are to capture it. How? That's easy…by words. To be precise, by speaking out loud the Word of God. <u>You cannot continue to think a thought and talk out loud at the same time. It cannot be done.</u> Try it. Your mind will shut up to see what your mouth is saying. Every time!

You have to stop the thoughts. Don't just sit there and THINK. The longer you think about a negative thought the more negative thoughts will come. After a while you will develop a pattern of thinking and before you know it you will have a stronghold in your mind against the Word of God. That's when we begin to walk in deception.

In the space below write a promise to yourself to practice the above discipline consistently for three days. The moment you have a negative thought immediately speak out loud a positive counterpart.

_____

_____

_____

_____

_____

_____

_____

Do not be conformed to this world but be transformed (changed) by the (entire) renewal of your mind (soul) by it's new ideals and it's new attitude, so that you can prove (for yourselves) what is the good and acceptable and perfect will of God. Romans 12: 2 AMP

Meditation for Week Nine

Ephesians 5:1-14 (Up Close and Personal)

This is Father calling us to a Higher Life.

Beloved,

I want you to follow My example in everything you do...just like a well loved child should.

Learn to act like Me. The more time you spend with Me the easier it will be. Mostly what I do is Love. When you keep company with Me you learn the Love Life.

And follow the example Christ left you. He loved you so much He gave Himself as a sacrifice to take away your sin. Christ's love for you was like sweet perfume to Me. I was pleased to say the least. His love was totally unselfish.

Do not use your mouth for dirty stories, foul talk, gossip, off colored jokes, or silly conversations, you have a higher use for your mouth... like prayer and praise. Use your tongue to create beauty andgood into your world. Remind each other of all My promises.

You can be sure that 'Heaven on Earth' or 'Heaven to Come' will never belong to anyone who is greedy or uses people for what they can get out of them. That form of idolatry will get you no-where fast…and certainly no-where near the Golden Dream in My Heart for you.

Don't let yourself be taken in by religious smooth talk. Don't be fooled by people who try to excuse these sins…for My wrath is upon them…and nothing good can get anywhere near them. Don't do these things and don't associate with Christians who act like that.

Once you walked around in a dark fog, but no more! You are full of Me! You are full of Light! Because of that, your behavior should show it. The bright Light in you makes your way plain. No more stumbling around. Your heart now is turned to what is good and right and true…these are the actions of a Child of Mine.

Learn as you go along what pleases Me. You can be sure I will let you know if you mess up. Take no part in the worthless pleasures of darkness and evil…but instead stand like a beacon in a dark place exposing their sin to the light of the Word. When you life stands in sharp contrast to their darkness, some of them will realize the error of their ways and want to walk in the Glorious Light of our Family. Our message to them is 'Awake, O Sleeper. and rise up from the grave and Christ will give you LIFE!'

And so Beloved Child of my heart SHINE!

I Love You, Father

Week Nine

The Kingdom of Excuses

~

It's a sad day when you find out that it's not accident or time or
fortune but just yourself that has kept things from you..

Lillian Hellman

~

How many years, and how many detours does
it take to derail a dream?

~

Excuses…the lies we tell ourselves.

~

Week Nine Assignments

When you hear, 'Jump and the net will appear.' What is your first reaction? Be honest...

_____

_____

_____

_____

_____

Perhaps you wrote, "Easy for you to say". Actually it's not easy for me to say...I've done it. Free falling is not easier than parachuting. But I can say... the net was there.

So what color is your parachute? Are you living your best Life? If not...why not? Write the answers ...

_____

_____

_____

_____

_____

_____

_____

_____

_____

_____

_____

_____

One thing about parachutes, they don't stop the fall...they just prolong the trip.

About your Morning Pages...are you doing them every morning? Why not? Do they seem useless to you? Silly? Could that be your soul giving it's opinion? If so, wonder what it is trying to hide? Don't bail out on *your Morning Pages.* Do them first thing every morning...three pages of whatever.

Reminder

DO NOT SHARE YOUR MORNING PAGES.

WHAT YOU WRITE IS STRICTLY BETWEEN YOU
AND FATHER!

Are you finding yourself Practicing His Presence at odd times… not only in the designated time slot? That's a good thing…like when your cooking dinner…watching TV…vacuuming...He really is there you know.

Are you adding minutes every week to your time with Father? If you have added five minutes a week since we began this Journey nine weeks ago, you aught to be spending fifty minutes each day *Practicing His Presence*. Part of that time could be spent reading *His Love Letters* to you…His Word…*Up Close and Personal.*

Such as: Hebrews 13: 5 b-6

My Precious Daughter…I will not in any way fail You… nor give You up… nor leave You without. support. I will not, I will not, I will not in any degree leave You helpless…nor forsake… nor let You down or relax My hold on You...Assuredly not!

So take comfort and be encouraged and confidently and boldly say, 'My Father is My helper; I will not be seized with alarm…I will not fear…or dread…or be terrified. What can mere man do to me?

Read the Word aloud…*Create with your mouth what you are reading with your eyes.*

A Postscript:

God is not going to do anything about our miserable circumstances.
Jesus did it all. (Past tense)
Our part is in trusting that if I step out on His Word
Even if I can't see it, the net will be there.

Meditation for Week Ten

Ephesians 5: 15-33 (Up Close and Personal)

Here are more personal instructions from our Father.

Beloved,

To pick up where I left off in last weeks letter…you really need to watch your step. I don't want you to stumble like the people who live in darkness. I want you to make the best use of your time because the days are evil. I want you to utilize the wisdom I have for you. You cannot afford to be reckless in your decisions…you must find out My will for your life. I want you to have discernment, understanding and knowledge.

Don't use wine (or anything else) to get high on. Excesses of anything lead to sin. You need to be continually be being filled with My Holy Spirit. Drink deeply of Him. Everyday be aware of His impartation into you life. Let the Spirit stimulate your soul. Get high on the Dream in My Heart for you. Express the joy you find in Me, in songs, and hymns, and spiritual songs. Express this wonderful joy to others. Let everyone see how thankful you are to have Me for your Father...do this in the Name of Jesus. (Actually you are not doing this for Me, I created praise and thanksgiving to help YOU defeat your enemies.)

About this submission thing...Out of honor to Christ I want My children to submit to one another. Look out for each other's good. Don't just think how a relationship can add to your life...think about how knowing you will bless other people. As a wife you must learn to adapt to your husband, as you submit to Me. This only means that your security in Me will overflow in love for your husband. I gave My daughters husbands so they could be loved and cared for as Christ cares for the Church.

Wives should love and support their husbands just as Christ loves and supports the Church. He gave the Church everything...it was a loved marked by giving, not getting. Christ's love makes the church whole. His words evokes her beauty. Everything He does and says is designed to bring the best out of her.

When a husband treats his wife like that he is doing himself a great favor. Then it will be easy for her to treat him with respect, reverence, regard, honor, esteem, praise, love, and admiration. It's a win-win situation. This kind of love walk, will create 'Days of Heaven on Earth' for my Family. That's My will for you. You do your part and I will do Mine.

I Really Love You, Father

Week Ten

The Kingdom of the Unresolved

What's Up With That?

Traveling toward *Peace*

Means traveling to Wholeness

It means being *Centered*

Not re-active…just responsive

Doing well and almost there

Something strange happens

I find I am running backwards

Stymied…perplexed…confused

What's up with this…

I am not that person…

Where did she come from…

The past is present …

Again…

Week Ten Assignments

This is the week to ask, 'What's Up With That?' Cut yourself no slack. No matter how long it takes; get to the bottom of every negative reaction.

Confronting the Issues: Possible Reactions to double-check... what comes out of me when the following buttons are pushed? Record you answers ...

Traffic is impossible and I'm late…

_____

_____

_____

The children just got on my last nerve…

_____

_____

_____

My husband snapped my last nerve…

_____

_____

_____

My mom, dad, husband, anybody…tries to lay a guilt trip on me…

_____

_____

_____

My boss treats me unfairly. I didn't get the raise…promotion…etc…

_____

_____

_____

A sales person or wait staff doesn't know the meaning of customer service…

_____

_____

_____

You waited six weeks for a special order and they sent the wrong size, color, style…

_____

_____

_____

The preacher say's something that goes against your pre-conceived, pre-programmed idea of 'whatever'…

_____

_____

_____

_____

You get put on hold for thirty minutes and then disconnected…

_____

_____

_____

You are believing God for the rent money and it's late…

_____

_____

_____

Concerning the latter…Father knows it is more important for us to realize what issues in our souls need attention than for Him to supply demands on our time schedules. Rent money is no problem to God. He does and will "…supply all our needs according to the riches in Glory by Christ Jesus." Trust me…that is some kind of serious riches. There is no lack. Abundance is one of His names…El Shaddai means "The God That Is More Than Enough." So 'Father More Than Enough' has a million ways to get you rent money…but if there is a problem in our souls that caused the lack we will run back up on the same problem again and again…month after month… year after year. Do you see how that can happen?

_____

_____

_____

Better to get the root fixed than specializing in trying to fix bad fruit. What is in us will manifest in our lives. This week we are inspecting fruit…and pulling up roots.

Note any other 'buttons' you detected. After confronting the Reaction simply ask Father to heal in your soul whatever the basic problem is…He will

_____

_____

_____

_____

_____

_____

_____

Is spending time *Practicing His Presence* easier now? If you have added five minutes to each day during our *Journey* you will be spending fifty minutes 'consciously' enjoying His company…on the *Morning Pages* as well as when ever He (or you) wants to talk.

Wonderful side effect of spending *Time in the Presence*: We have a tendency to act and even look like *Who* we hang around with. The folks in Jesus' day looked at the disciples and "…saw that they had been with Jesus." Remember….

To keep a lamp burning

we have to keep putting oil in it.

Mother Teresa

Do Morning Pages…Continually remind yourself that these are just another form of meditation…they will locate exactly where our souls are daily. Yes, this exercise cost something (time…discipline) but you and your future are worth it.

You have a *Full of* Beauty *Life* waiting for you. The whole *Plan* is in your human spirit and once our spirit is in charge…the *Plan* will unfold. Note a few of the dreams you may have hidden in your heart. What would do if there were no obstacles?

_____

_____

_____

_____

_____

_____

_____

_____

_____

_____

Meditation for Week Eleven

Ephesians 6:1-10 (Up Close and Personal)

This letters covers the way Father wants us to treat people.

Beloved,

Children should obey their parents. If you teach your children to obey you, they will have an easier time obeying Me when the time comes. This is the first commandment with a promise. Obedience will bring to them (and you) a long prosperous life. If you personally honor your parents (not because they deserve it), but as an honor to me… I will honor you with a wonderful Full-of-Peace life. A long, full life of prosperity.

Parents should never irritate their children and make them angry. Be wise. Be kind. Don't over correct them until they lose the reality of your love. I don't treat you that way…so don't treat your children that way. When you were born again into My Family, I became your role model as a parent. Treat children the way I treat you. Take them by the hand and lead them in the way that is right …full of love and mercy.

If you are working a job for another be honorable. Do everything with singleness of heart, eager to please them. Don't just work hard when you know the boss is watching. Let your motive be to please Me. As a partner in the Family Business of Love you actually work for Me and Jesus. So everyday think of your job as being on My payroll. Do your work heartily, with good will. Remember Beloved, whatever good you do I will see it, and I will repay you. I see everything…and I pay well.

Now, if you have people working under you…follow the same principle. Don't threaten, or abuse folks with the words you speak. Remember I love them too…and however you treat people will come back on you. So act like who you are… 'My Child'. Be wise, kind, just, and thoughtful. Let everyone around you see by the way you treat them, that, in your life…Love rules.

Beloved, in closing, remember to be strong in Me. Empower yourself in our relationship. As we spend more and more time together you will take on My energy and strength. I have boundless resources for you. These resources enable you to live a life of purpose and power. By taking hold of everything I have for you… you cannot fail.

Love Forever, Father

Week Eleven

The Kingdom of Death

Spread love everywhere you go: first of all in your own house...let no one ever come to you without leaving better or happier. Be the living expression of God's kindness; kindness in your face, kindness in your eyes, kindness in your warm greeting.

Mother Teresa

~

The acid test of true Christianity is...
Are you fun to live with?"

~

Week Eleven Assignments

So, did this Kingdom step on your toes? Honesty is the only policy. If so, just ask for forgiveness…it's over just that quick.

_____

_____

_____

_____

_____

_____

So, 'Are you fun to life with?' Answer honestly… you could ask your nearest and dearest for the answer to that question…but you no doubt already know the answer. Are you..?

_____

_____

_____

_____

_____

_____

_____

_____

In your time with Father this week sincerely ask him to do for you, what David asked Him to do in **Psalm 139**…

"Search me thoroughly O God, and know MY heart! Try me and know my thoughts! See if there is any wicked or hurtful way in me. And lead me in to the way everlasting."

Continue your Morning Pages. Have you discovered the 'page and a half secret' yet? Many of us who are dedicated *Morning Pages* addicts discovered that the first page and a half of the three pages are just 'stuff' we need to get out of the way and out of our mind before we start the day. The second half is the 'good stuff' from a soul set free and sometimes straight from Father's Heart delivered with clarity from our spirits. Remember, *"One Word from God can change your life forever."*

He is always speaking …are we listening?

A Note from Father given to us by Jesus in John 16:13-14

"The Spirit of Truth (the Holy Spirit) has come. You can fully expect Him to take you by the hand and guide you into all Truth there is.

He will tell you everything He has been told about your life.

He takes of the knowledge that is in Me so He can reveal it to you.

He will literally tell you what is coming up in the future…everything He says will bring honor to Me…so pay attention."

Up Close and Personal

you matter.

We mold one another's
dreams. We hold each other's
fragile hopes in our hands.
We all touch others' hearts.
We must do this with wisdom.
And Love......

Meditation for Week Twelve

At the end of our Journey we will finish out
The Book of Ephesians 6:11-24 (Up Close and Personal.)

This is a final prayer for Father's help in making
His Word a reality in our lives.

Beloved Father,

I come to You in the Name of my Savior Jesus…please teach me about the armor you have given me. I want to put on and wear the whole armor. I want to wear all the weapons in Your armory, so that I can successfully resist all the devil methods. I know satan has strategies to deceive me, and I can't fight him in the natural.

I must have the armor of the Spirit realm to fight these spirits that come from the very headquarters of evil…and have rule over the darkness that is in the world (and in the darkness resident in my soul) I know Father that without help from You I am up against far more than I can handle.

Therefore I desire to take up, and wear all You have provided for me in the way of armor and weapons. I want to receive Your power to withstand the evil, and having done all the crises demands I want to be found standing solidly in my place…in You.

I am learning Father, that Truth, Righteousness, Peace, Faith, Salvation, and the Word are more than religious words. They are the armor and the weapons that will ensure my victory over all the attacks of my enemy. They are the weapons of my warfare. The belt of Truth means I will be honest in all my dealings. Honest with You, honest with others, honest with myself. I will know the truth and the truth will set me free from satan's agendas.

The breastplate of Righteousness will enable me to walk in total integrity…in right standing with You. When I stand in Peace, I have firm-footed stability to face my enemy. *The Gospel of Peace* will be manifested wherever I walk. The Gospel of Peace is Your Word and I will be ready and prompt to tell people about Your Love.

Above all this Father, I want to lift up the mighty shield of Faith… Faith in You…Faith in the sacrifice of Jesus…Faith in Your Word. With this shield I know not one dart, or missile from satan can get any where near me.

I want the helmet of total Salvation to cover my mind (soul). Salvation covers a multitude of promises and I want to have my thinking saturated with all of them. So that, when satan comes against my mind he will hit a covering of Salvation.

And Father, teach me how to use the sword of Your Word...to cut off, keep back, and slay satan's plans against me. A sword can also be used to cut a path through a dense jungle of overgrowth; thank you for teaching me how to use your Word to cut through the jungle in my soul and for bringing me into a beautiful land of clear thinking.

I love the way I have learned to Practice Your Presence and to be in contact with You 24/7. This must be what Paul was talking about when he told the Ephesians to pray at all times, on every occasion, in every season, in the Spirit. To simply live every moment in Your Presence...talking to You about whatever the Holy Spirit leads me to say.

I pray now for my brothers and sisters in the Family of God...help me to be a blessing and an inspiration to others...help us to grow together in love and unity. Help us to be quick to mend broken hearts and to walk in such gentleness and kindness that no one anywhere can say the Body of Christ is anything but LOVE.

For Your ministers...our leaders...the ones on the front lines of the war against satan, I pray that they will have boldness to speak Your Word in power and might, in order to turn the ones Jesus died for into the Light of Your Love. I pray each one will know exactly what to say and speak it at just the right time.

Father, I cannot thank You enough for the Peace and Love, and Faith...You, and the Lord Jesus gave me. I love My Lord Jesus Christ and I Love You. I know without a doubt my Beloved Father, that my whole spirit, soul, and body is covered in Your Grace, Your undeserved favor…because I love Jesus…and I do so love Him.

Forever, Your Child _____

Morning came today slipping
From the fingers of God
It lay white and still outside my window
Waiting to be filled...
With dreams and visions

Wanda G.

Week Twelve

The Kingdom of Focus

The Journey of a Soul

I walked through life finding no one

To affirm my deepest self

I felt ideas inside me so mystical

So intense…that at times

I hesitated to blink for fear they would fade

Caught up in mediocrity of endless days

I was drowning living as 'they' expected me to

I could not…would not accept that nothingness

As ' My Life' in the heart of Father

I knew…somewhere…someway...somehow

There must be rendering off of impurities

That covered my gift…my dreams…myself

There was a world of wholeness inside of me

One step into Reality and I knew it was there

I longed…ached…hungered for it's wonder

I knew I could find it…and when I did

My heart would Journey to a place called Peace

Week Twelve Assignments:

Record five 'life altering' concepts you have discovered on your Journey.

_____

_____

_____

_____

_____

_____

Record what you intend to do with the information you now own. Remember 'information' alone will not bring change...but a Quality Decision to put into practice said information...day after day...will change everything.

_____

_____

_____

_____

_____

_____

_____

Your time in His Presence aught to be an hour a day by now… thirty minutes on the *Morning Pages*…thirty minutes just with Him.

Go back and read your Morning Pages. Take a highlighter and highlight the parts that you feel came from Him…through your spirit …through your renewed soul. This again, will take practice…but He is there to help you.

Draw a large circle in your Notebook. Inside the circle write a dream Father has placed in Your heart. It may be a business…a ministry…a book to write…a song to sing…a work of art…a school you want to go to…a job you want…a new career…a nice home…a Godly mate…a daddy for your fatherless children…whatever is the desire of your heart.

Outside the circle write the names of suspected 'Wet Blankets'. You know who they are…if you are not sure…ask the Holy Spirit. He is there to lead you and guide you into all the 'Truth'. If you feel a 'caution' like a yellow flashing light in your 'inner man' (spirit)… pay attention…proceed carefully.

Inside the circle write the name, or names of people who are not in the 'Wet Blanket Ministry'. These are kindred souls…they will share the Dream. Don't wrap your self in a 'Wet Blanket'

Wrap yourself and your Dream…In Peace…in the Word…Wrap yourself in Father's Love.

Whatever you do…Don't reach for your nearest and dearest 'Wet Blanket'.

Do not tolerate anyone who tries to throw water on your newly lighted flame. Forget good intentions. Forget they didn't mean it. Set your focus and set your boundaries.

Let the Morning bring me word of your
unfailing love, O Lord, for I have put my
trust in you. Show me the way I should go,
for to you I lift up my soul.

Psalm 143:8 NIV

A Bit More Inspiration

"Don't say you don't have enough time. You have exactly the same number of hours per day that were given to Helen Keller, Pasteur, Michaelangelo, Mother Teresea, Leonardo da Vinci, Thomas Jefferson, and Albert Einstein."

Life's Little Instruction Book, compiled by H. Jackson Brown, Jr

The Wise Woman's Stone

"A wise woman who was traveling in the mountains found a precious stone in a stream. The next day she met another traveler who was hungry, and the wise woman opened her bag to share her food. The hungry traveler saw the precious stone and asked the woman to give it to him. She did so without hesitation.

The traveler left, rejoicing in his good fortune. He knew the stone was worth enough to give him security for a lifetime. But a few days later he came back to return the stone to the wise woman.

"I've been thinking," he said, "I know how valuable the stone is, but I give it back in the hope that you can give me something even more precious. Give me what you have within you that enabled you to give me the stone." **Author Unknown**

"Your life is your garden, your thoughts are your seeds. If your life isn't awesome. Then you've been watering the weeds."

DON'T QUIT

When things go wrong, as they sometimes will,
When the road you're trudging seems all uphill,
When the funds are low and the debts are high,
And you want to smile, but you have to sigh,
When care is pressing you down a bit.
Rest, if you must, but don't you quit!

Life is strange with its twists and turns,
As every one of us sometimes learns,
And many a failure turns about,
when he might have won had he stuck it out;
Don't give up though the pace seems slow-
You may succeed with another blow.

Often the goal is nearer than,
It seems to a faint and faltering man,
Often the struggler has given up,
When he might have captured the victor's cup,
And he learned too late when the night slipped down,
How close he was to the golden crown.

Success is failure turned inside out-
The silver tint of the clouds of doubt,
And you never can tell how close you are,
It may be near when it seems so far,
So stick to the fight when you're hardest hit--
It's when things seem worst that you must not quit.

Unknown

Author Wanda Winters-Gutierrez creates books specializing in creative non-fiction, inspiration, and memoirs.

She is known as a writer with a unique ability to draw the reader into the emotion of the moment. Because of her insight and spiritual understanding she is able to touch the hearts and souls of emotionally wounded people all over the world.

She leads workshops, seminars, retreats, teaching meditation, meditative journaling, and other creative classes. Her various endeavors are all geared toward setting people free from the unresolved issues of their past and empowering them to go beyond to a lovely future.

Her books are recommended by counselors and therapist; used in prisons, halfway houses, as well as shelters for abused women, book clubs and as study guides in assorted woman's organizations.

Other Books by Wanda G.

Moving On... An Excerpt

"Imagine we are sitting at my kitchen table. I have poured you a hot cup of coffee, or tea if you prefer. There may even be a plate of warm cookies nearby.

We talk and laugh, perhaps shed a few tears. As I take your hand in mine and look into your eyes I want you to realize that no matter what the present circumstances are... 'Happiness' is your destination, and 'Choice' is your passport.

I tell you upfront I have only one message... "While I celebrate your survival, I know for sure it is only a launching pad for your beautiful future. You have within you all you need to begin again. God has much more for you and you can take the first step today."

Moving On... is about acknowledging 'what is' and making quality decisions to move on to 'what can be.' This book is about change and choices. It is about a new beginning in all areas of life.

They say that the books that really change a reader's life are those that change the author's as well. In this collection of articles, book excerpts, poetry,and quotes I share my heart.

I pray they will give you the inspiration for your journey as they did mine. Moving On... follows my personal journey into the world of survivors from the early days until now. It is a world of pain and beauty, hopelessness and healing, death and new life.

Family Secrets: & *The Reunion* is co-author *Grace Ann Neuharth's* true story. *Family Secrets* includes murder, suicide, abuse, depression, addictions and slavery. *The Reunion* deals with the long range effects of those kind of tragedies on families as they reunited with loved ones.

FROM Family Secrets: Letters to my Granddaughters:

"The sexual abuse started when I was very young, too young to know what it was and too terrified to tell. One day when everyone else was out of the house, he told me to come into his room and lay on his bed with him. When I hesitated, he said, "I am your daddy now, and if you don't want to end up like your mother, you better just do what I tell you to do....That's when I saw the knife lying on the nightstand.""

From **The Reunion:** An Adopted Childs Letters to a Missing Mother

Dear Mom...If I could have written you letters during the early years they may have looked like this.....
Mommy-Mommy please come and get me! I want to go home. I do not know who these people are. They tell me that they are my mommy and daddy but I don't think they are. The boy, who they call David, seems to be their real son. They called me Marilyn Sue and I hate it.

Mom... these people do mean things to me. The man hurts me... he has a big knife. Sometimes I wake up at night scared. I don't like that. I want to stop being hurt. Please, please come and get me. Please...

More about Family Secrets @ facebook.com/BooksByWandaG
The Reunion can be found @ createspace.com/3677024

The Search for Peace:A Woman's Guide to Spiritual Wholeness

Take a tender and healing Journey through the pages of *The Search for Peace.* Here you will discover how to overcome personal fears and reach emotional wholeness. You will be guided beyond walls of pain and brokenness into true freedom.

Part self-help book, part workbook, The Search for Peace guides you through inner healing and helps show you how to allow God to renew your mind that you may see yourself as He sees you—loved, capable and whole.
Wanda Winters-Gutierrez possesses the brave honesty to share episodes of her own emotional brokenness and challenged past. She had spent her entire life discovering the wholeness that only God can bring. She will show you how to experience this too!

A Whole-Woman Revolution is in progress...The Search for Peace is one of the handbooks.

Wherever books are sold..

She decided to free herself, dance into the wind, create a new language. And birds fluttered around her, writing "yes" into the sky.

Excerpt from a Work in Progress

Mountain Man: Memoir of a Free Spirit

By Wanda Winters-Gutierrez

For a moment imagine you have come to visit Harvey on his mountain. You may have read about him, heard stories, or met him somewhere on his travels. To get there you have followed highway 70 up from historic Rogersville, Tennessee.

It is early morning and for most of the 17 miles, you find yourself driving through a cloud. A misty fog decended on the mountain during the night settling gently into the valleys. Occasionally, when a window in the mist clears, you glimpse the Great Smokies spilling away into the horizon; it is hard to tell where the mountains end and the heavens begin.

Eventually you emerge from the winding switch back curves of the highway and begin to pass roads, hollows, creeks, and communities with names such as Frog Level, Little Pumpkin Valley, Turkey Creek, Copper Ridge, and a church named 'Compromise'.

You turn at Gravely Valley Road and follow it until you find a certain mail box. The entry into Harvey's land grew over long ago for lack of use, so you pull into his neighbor's driveway. You were told it is okay to park your car inside the gate; you will walk the rest of the way. The neighbor's property is cleared farmland surrounded by forest; his house is barely visible behind a stand of pines farther up the drive. To the left, along the woods, a logging company has ripped a narrow road into the mountain. It looks straight uphill and you will have to climb it.

Harvey's cabin is two or three miles farther on. Stepping out of the car the mountain wraps your senses. You hear the creek rushing over rocks as it follows its century old path around lower border of the mountain. The air is crisp. Somewhere over on the next farm a rooster crows. Nearby a blue jay calls out a welcome...or a warning.

You start walking. Twenty minutes later you stop to catch your breath and look back at your car a half-mile away; it is the last symbol of civilization you will see for a while. Walking on, still uphill, you remember to check your cell phone...no bars. You are now officially separated from the outside world.

You are on the lookout for a large rock where you are to turn left and cross onto Harvey's land. Another 15 minutes, past a bend or two in the road an outcropping of layered sandstone appears. It looks as if it may hover over the entrance to a buried cave and it is big. To the left of the rock a barbed wire fence stretches on up the mountain and defines the north boundary line of the sixty acres. Hanging on the fence is a hand carved wooden sign, "Road Closed: No Motorized Vehicles Allowed." Welcome to Harvey's world.

Climbing the fence, you follow the path through damp woods of pine, oak, poplar. Branches create a laced canopy above your head. Jewel-like dewdrops glisten on grasses and the tips of pine needles. The trail is quiet except for the soft crackle of twigs under your feet and an occasional chattering of a squirrel. As you walk farther into the mountain the world shrinks to the path before you. Moss, rocks, ferns, leaves take on exquisite details you would have missed on other walks in wide-open spaces.

The pervading silence of the mountain brings with it solitude humans rarely experience. Alone? Not really, forest eyes are wondering at the stranger who suddenly appeared in their kingdom. Standing still for a moment you see a whitetail-deer no farther than a stone's throw away. She solemnly stares at you with unblinking eyes then melts off into the morning mist.

Moving on at a gentler pace you vaguely wonder what it would be like to live this close to God's creatures and yet not see another human being for weeks at a time. You have heard that before settling here Harvey traversed the length and breadth of the country with only a backpack. What kind of person chooses to endure heat and cold, rain and snowstorms, loneliness and uncomfortable beds, or no bed, and danger...for what? A sunset? Another mountain, new people...freedom...solitude? There has to be a story behind the Hermit of the Mountain. Somehow you feel deep within that he may have answers that will help you live your own live in a more authentic way. That is why you made this journey.

The scent of burning wood causes you to pause and look around. Faintly, through the trees, you see a cabin nestled in a dip of the mountain. As you get closer you notice a hazy trail of smoke rising from the pipe in the roof and floating off toward the creek. The window glows with the warmth of a coal oil lamp...this has to be the place.

Right about here is where you start second-guessing your decision. Now what? Just how does one make an unannounced visit to a hermit? You have heard he is friendly, but he obviously lives alone for a reason. What if he doesn't like company? Wonder if he has a gun? Didn't someone tell you that everybody in Tennessee has a gun? Still not sure you finally just move past the questions and walk down the hill calling out! "Hello! Anybody home?"

He steps around the corner of the cabin, a short stocky man dressed in a faded flannel shirt and worn jeans. His kind, yet intensely blue eyes gaze at you from behind wired rimmed glasses above a Grizzly Adams beard. As you step into the clearing he says, "Welcome friend..." and extends his hand. He asks your name and where you are from and an with old-school graciousness he invites you into his home.

Stepping inside the first thing you encounter is possibly the largest collection of books you have ever seen outside a public library. Books are everywhere. Floor to ceiling they line the walls, the shelves, the rafters. They are stacked on tables, chairs, windowsills and on the floor. A library of this magnitude is the last thing you ex

On closer inspection you will find they categorized by subject...poetry, novels, history, medicine, law, how-to, self-help, biographies, science, nature, art, religion, theology, mysteries, politics and literally every other subject from anthropology to zoology. Homer's Iliad rest beside Thoreau. Shakespeare, Tolstoy, Emerson, Hemingway, Steinbeck, Thurber, and Twain share a whole section. James Patterson, and other modern day writers find their place near an entire set of Encyclopedia Britannica which were given to him by the Britannica Company when he did a story telling event for them.

Overwhelmed by the book's sheer numbers, your unspoken questions tumble over themselves... "How many are there? Has he read them all? How did he get them up here?" Later, when you get to know him better, you ask and he answers with a chuckle, "Not real sure about how many...lost count years ago...maybe about 10,000 here and more in the other cabin. Yes, I've read them all, so

It is evident your host is totally at ease with his surroundings. Offering no apology for the simplicity of his lifestyle, and with all the dignity of a well-to-do Victorian gentleman showing you into his parlor, he invites you to have a seat at the oilcloth-covered table. More than likely you will be sitting in a chair he made from a tree on the property. The books and warm hospitality have already knocked many of your preconceived ideas of a mountain man in the head, but more surprises wait.

He is soft spoken, possesses a quick wit, ready laughter, and delightful sense of humor. His disarming way of laying out the most profound statement wrapped in a smile can be intriguing. For instance, when you inquire about his decision to live out-side-the-box, he replies, "It just came to me one day that a human's life must have purpose, at least to the person living it." While you are digesting that nugget he adds a few pieces of wood to the stove, throws some strange looking bark into a pot of water and asked you if you have ever had sassafras tea?

As the morning progresses the range of subjects cover everything from the origin and nesting habits of the songbird singing a pure, heartfelt melody outside the window, to quantum physics verses Einstein's theory of relativity. Obviously behind his deceptive simplicity is a well-educated man. When you ask him what University he studied at, he grins and motions toward the bookshelves..."An illness in my childhood kept me from attending school for any extended period of time. I only went through 4th grade. The family doctor told me that if I was ever going to have any sort of education, I should not only read, but learn to 'love to read' "Read anything you can get your hands on…even if it is comic books, just read." So, I read."

A natural storyteller in the old Appalachian tradition you could listen for hours as he shares mountain stories and songs that he learned from his grandpa, as well as the accounts of his adventures during the decade he hopped freights, hitchhiked, and walked through thirty-eight states and two countries. He admits he has a few bad experiences, but mostly met some good people and made many friends.

Before your visit is over you will be fully convinced that the old ways are best...freight trains are a really an interesting way to travel...living in the woods by yourself is exactly what you want to do...and taking the hardships you encounter in life and using them for stepping stones makes perfect sense.

You will be ready to do as Ralph Waldo Emerson suggested, and Harvey did, *"Do not go where the path may lead, go instead where there is no path and leave a trail."*

Mountain Man will be available in 2012

www.ingramcontent.com/pod-product-compliance
Lightning Source LLC
Chambersburg PA
CBHW032102280526
45784CB00013B/2944